TEXT AND
PHOTOGRAPHS
Howard Hall

SERIES EDITOR
Vicki León

DESIGN
Ashala Nicols-Lawler

ADDITIONAL
PHOTOGRAPHS
Mark D. Conlin

SAY IT WITH COLOR:
from the fancy fish
headdress of a blenny
(far right) to the color-
crayon brightness of
a tiny Spanish shawl
nudibranch and its
anemone neighbors,
kelp forest animals
often advertise
aggression or inedibility
with color and frills.

SILVER BURDETT PRESS

© 1995 Silver Burdett Press
Published by Silver Burdett Press.
A Simon & Schuster Company
299 Jefferson Road,
Parsippany, NJ 07054
d in the United States of America

Contents

The KELP FOREST

CLOSE-UP
A Focus on Nature

SILVER BURDETT PRESS
© 1995 Silver Burdett Press
Published by Silver Burdett Press.
A Simon & Schuster Company
299 Jefferson Road, Parsippany, NJ 07054
Printed in the United States of America

Library of Congress
Cataloging-in-Publication Data
Hall, Howard, 1949–
  The kelp forest:the ebb and flow of life in the
sea's richest habitat/by Howard Hall;photographs
by Howard Hall.
      p. cm. -- (Close up)
    ISBN 0-382-24863-5 (LSB) 10 9 8 7 6 5 4 3 2 1
    ISBN 0-382-24864-3 (SC)   10 9 8 7 6 5 4 3 2
    1. Kelp bed ecology--Juvenile literature.
  2. Kelps--Juvenile literature. [1.Kelp bed ecology.
  2. Kelps. 3. Marine animals. 4. Ecology.] I. Title
  II. Series: Close up (Parsippany, N.J.)
  QH541.5.K4H35   1994
  574.5'2636--dc20   94-31823
                                                  CIP
                                                  AC

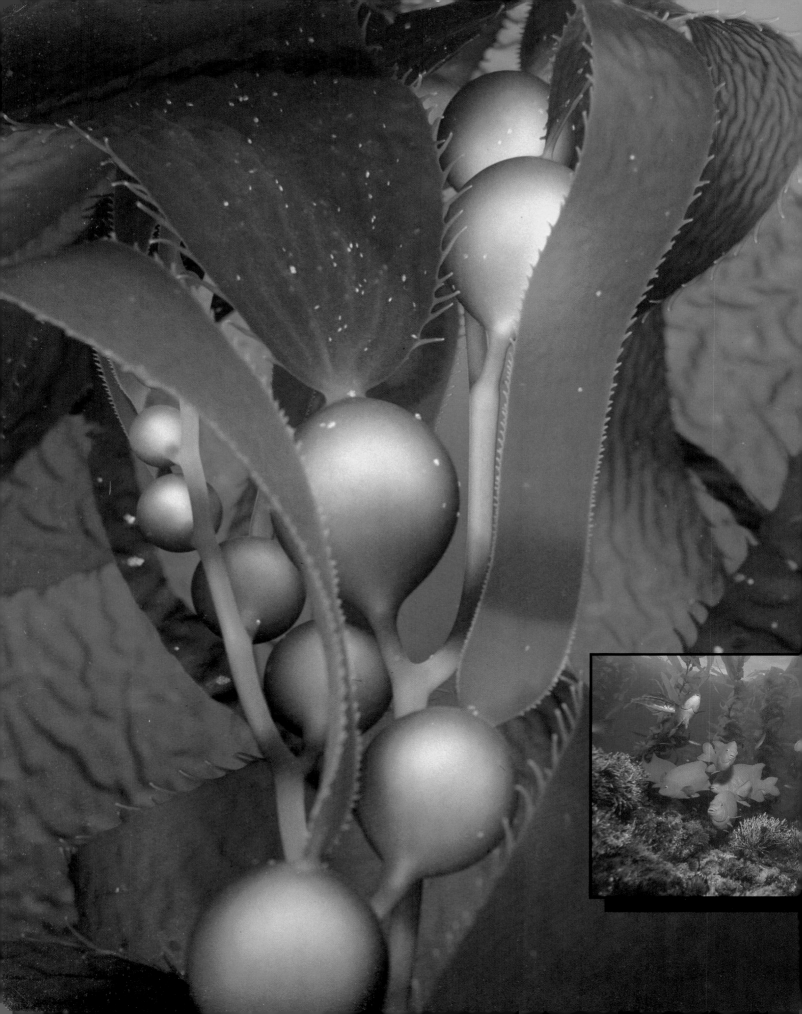

A great golden wilderness

O f all the forests that exist on Planet Earth, only one is entirely alien to humans. No ancient culture ever lived beneath the sheltering canopy of this forest. No bird sings here. No flower blooms. No wind blows. Yet this airless, flowerless place teems with animals and lush vegetation. This is the kelp forest, an amber wilderness beneath the sea.

Until 1943 and the invention of self-contained underwater diving apparatus, few humans had ever seen the riches of this habitat. Once SCUBA divers began to slip beneath the ocean's surface, they saw winged creatures that were not birds. They marveled at brilliantly colored blossoms that were not flowers. They found creatures never before seen by humans. And they encountered leviathans that filled them with terror. They entered a forest of dim golden light, as crowded with life as any tropical rainforest and as full of wonders.

Ironically, these vast stands of marine forest hug coastal shorelines, often just a stone's throw away from cities, highways, and human activity. But few humans are aware of kelp forests, or even know exactly what kelp is. To coastal residents, the word kelp conjures up a pungent, brown mass of seaweed washed up on the beach. To fishermen and boating enthusiasts, kelp represents a marine obstacle, a vegetative mass that often fouls boat propellers.

The true nature of this wonderful plant can only be seen beyond the surfline, where living kelp flourishes. These undersea forests are both refuge and hunting ground for countless fishes, invertebrates, marine

HOLDING FAST:
With its fingerlike haptera, a kelp plant clings to rocks or other solid objects on the bottom. So tenacious is its grip that rock will break before the holdfast will. Like a tree's roots, the holdfast anchors the plant for five years or more. Fronds, on the other hand, are shed like leaves as often as twice a year.

mammals, and man. Ecologically and economically, the value of kelp forests rivals that of any forest found on land.

All large aquatic plants belong to one of three main groups or phyla of algae: red, green, or brown. Kelp belongs to the brown algae phylum. About 20 species of kelp thrive in the cooler waters along the Pacific Coast of North America. The largest species of these? *Macrocystis pyrifera* or giant kelp, the biggest aquatic plant in the world. It grows in water as deep as 130 feet, reaching all the way to the surface. These are the "trees" that form the kelp forest environment.

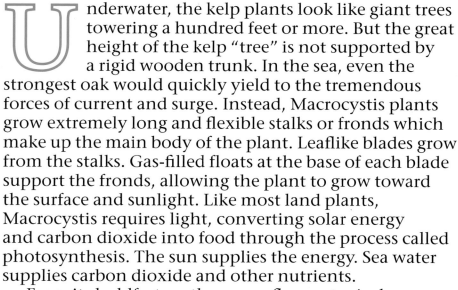

Unlike terrestrial plants, kelp plants get nourishment not from moisture and nutrients in the soil, but from seawater itself. Kelp plants have no root system. Instead, each kelp plant anchors itself to the rocky reef or substrate of the ocean floor by a holdfast. Intertwining rootlike structures called haptera securely glue the base of the plant to the rocky bottom. These haptera employ the world's strongest adhesive.

Underwater, the kelp plants look like giant trees towering a hundred feet or more. But the great height of the kelp "tree" is not supported by a rigid wooden trunk. In the sea, even the strongest oak would quickly yield to the tremendous forces of current and surge. Instead, Macrocystis plants grow extremely long and flexible stalks or fronds which make up the main body of the plant. Leaflike blades grow from the stalks. Gas-filled floats at the base of each blade support the fronds, allowing the plant to grow toward the surface and sunlight. Like most land plants, Macrocystis requires light, converting solar energy and carbon dioxide into food through the process called photosynthesis. The sun supplies the energy. Sea water supplies carbon dioxide and other nutrients.

From its holdfast on the ocean floor, a typical Macrocystis may grow more than 200 feet long, its fronds rising all the way to the surface from more than 100 feet below. Macrocystis is speedy, too. In fact, kelp rivals bamboo as one of the fastest-growing plants in the world. If you had a way of staying underwater all day, you could literally watch it grow. Fronds that have reached the surface where sunlight is plentiful may increase their length by as much as two feet per day. Once there, they continue to grow, mingling with other kelp plants to form a floating, dancing canopy over the forest.

COOL CUSTOMERS:
Brown algae like Macrocystis grows best in nutrient-rich waters where temperatures stay below 72° Fahrenheit. Pacific Coast kelp forests grow as far north as Alaska and as far south as Baja California. Along the coast of South America, kelp flourishes near Chile and Peru. Kelp stands can be found off the Atlantic coast from Cape Cod north, and near Argentina. Forests of other large kelp species ring the coasts of Southern Australia, New Zealand, Tasmania, South Africa, and many sub-Antarctic islands.

LIFE IN THE UPPER STORY:

The kelp forest canopy

O n the water's surface, the bobbing brown blades and bulbs of the kelp forest canopy give little hint of the beauty beneath. Just below the surface, the sun sends long shafts of light through the amber-colored fronds, softly illuminating a forest filled with life. Fish glide through the golden light in search of shelter among the kelp fronds. Crabs and mollusks climb the kelp, feeding upon other invertebrates and upon the kelp itself. And the reef at the base of the forest is alive with lobsters, anemones, snails, nudibranchs, and bottom-dwelling fishes. Hundreds of species of animals thrive beneath the kelp canopy, all part of the ecology of this habitat, all in some manner dependent upon the kelp itself.

Many animals feed directly on kelp plants. Fish such as opaleye eat Macrocystis fronds and other kelp. The Norris' top snail spends

Topside, the kelp forest canopy forms a bobbing raft of blades, convenient anchors for snoozing sea otters and their fluffy babies. From a distance, kelp masses sometimes look like log rafts or great oil slicks staining the water. How to tell the difference? Look and listen for signs of bird and animal life.

Who plucks urchins with its buck teeth?

The sheephead, a mild-mannered fish whose dental equipment gives it a risk-free way to nibble prickly, hard-to-open prey, such as crabs and sea urchins. Along with the sea otter, this fish keeps pesky urchin populations from chewing up the kelp forest. At least, it used to. Like the otter, the sheephead has become increasingly uncommon in its Pacific Coast range. All sheephead fishes begin life as females. Once they've reached about one-third of their full size of three feet or so, they look around to size up the available males. Then, with hermaphroditic ease, an appropriate number of females become males, changing color to advertise the fact. A territorial species, the sheephead's bright pink and black markings also serve to warn others off the turf.

much of its life climbing giant kelp plants while nibbling on the fronds. Once the snail reaches the top, it lets go and plummets to the bottom, where it seeks out another kelp tree and begins the rise-and-fall cycle once again.

Other invertebrates depend upon drift kelp for food. Kelp plants continually produce new fronds that grow toward the surface. Old fronds regularly break off and drift away to make room for new growth. This process is called sloughing. The discarded fronds either drift to shore and wash up on the beach or they sink to the bottom. Fronds that reach bottom don't last long. For many invertebrates, this drift kelp is breakfast, lunch, and dinner.

Abalone feed almost exclusively on drift kelp. This large, single-shelled mollusk has two prominent features: a rugged shell and a powerful muscle called a foot. The abalone uses its foot to grip the reef. The sturdy shell covers the animal, protecting it from predators. The ab spends most of its life in one spot, attached to the same rock. Here it waits for drift kelp to approach close enough so it can get a foothold.

To humans, abalones have long been valuable and sought-after for food. Divers harvest the mollusks by prying them free of the reef. To do so, they must use very strong pry bars. A diver can quickly break an expensive

PRICKLY DINNER:
Sheephead fishes (left) and bat stars (above) dine on urchins, but their techniques vary. Using tube feet, bat stars up-end urchins to get at the tender, unprotected parts. To reach into the recesses of the urchin's shell, bat stars athletically project their stomachs outside their leathery bodies.

Schooling fish often move in and out of the kelp forest, or patrol its edges. Why do fish such as jack mackerel school? Greater safety in numbers, for one thing. Sensing organs along their silvery sides help detect hungry foes and keep the school moving in unison. Schooling also provides more eyes to spot food. And it's a way of assuring that every jack mackerel meets a mate.

knife by trying to pop an abalone off a rock. When the frustrated diver swims away with a broken knife in his hand, he may have left the abalone to die. Abalone are hemophiliacs. Their blood does not clot. If the diver's knife cuts the abalone's flesh, the mollusk will probably bleed to death, fall off the rock, and be consumed by scavengers. The law requires ab divers to use pry bars with no sharp edges. That way, if an abalone measures below the minimum size, it can safely be replaced on the reef.

Largest of the seven species found on the Pacific Coast is the red abalone. The shell of a red may grow nearly 12 inches across, yielding up to a pound of delicious, high-priced meat. Despite the price the meat brings, few divers still make a living collecting abs. This mollusk has been severely over-fished, especially off the California coast.

Many divers have now switched to diving for red sea urchins. Largest of the half a dozen common species of urchin found in the kelp forest habitat, the red is only occasionally red as advertised. The great majority of baby red urchins grow up to be black. Unlike abalone, which has a ready market in the United States, most urchins are exported to Asian countries. Sushi aficionados consider the urchin's reproductive organs – usually called roe –

to be delicacies for which they are willing to pay dearly.

The kelp forest habitat provides shelter for hundreds of species of fishes and invertebrates. Many small species increase their chances of survival by remaining concealed within the dim light of the forest, or by taking refuge among the lush plant growth. Often, their predators find hunting in the kelp forest itself too restrictive, and concentrate their activities along the forest perimeter.

Blue sharks and mako sharks, for example, prefer the unrestricted freedom of the open ocean to the confines of the kelp forest. In the forest, prey can easily out-maneuver these large predators by dashing behind kelp fronds. So sharks wait at the outer edge of the kelp for inhabitants to venture out a little too far.

In the summer, large schooling fish like yellowtail and bonita migrate north into temperate waters, where they patrol the outer edge of the kelp forest. Great white sharks also pass along the forest's outside edge, keeping a watchful eye for seals and sea lions resting on the surface.

Harbor seals spend their days sleeping on coastal rocks or resting on the buoyant surface of the kelp canopy, safely concealed from sharks. During the night, however, they journey out into deeper waters, diving as much as 1,200 feet for fishes and squid.

Sea lions also hunt at night, spending their days playing in the kelp or basking in the sun along the rocky shoreline.

Sea lions love to show off. Few marine animals move as quickly or as gracefully. Although white sharks prefer sea lions as a diet item, they have little chance of catching one that is on its guard. In fact, sea lions often heckle a white shark as it patrols the sea lions' habitat. These sleek, doglike pinnipeds seem to enjoy testing their courage by diving down and nipping at the shark's tail or dorsal fin. The shark doesn't mind. He just keeps swimming back and forth along the outer edge of the forest. It may take days, but eventually the sea lions get careless. Eventually they forget there is a single-minded white shark about. Perhaps the sea lion decides to nap. Or it gets busy, barking at other sea lions on shore with its head out of the water. Its guard only needs to be down for a instant. In that moment, the shark's seemingly docile behavior changes. It suddenly switches directions, rushing upward and taking the sea lion in a flash of muscle and teeth.

Other, smaller predators make additional use of the kelp forest's possibilities for concealment and ambush. Kelpfish, for instance, are shaped and

colored to resemble kelp blades. When hiding among the fronds, they even move like the blades as the kelp sways in the surge. To the small fish hunted by the kelpfish, the predator is nearly invisible. Other enemies await also. Kelp rockfish, kelp bass, and other species lurk among the fronds, waiting for prey to pass within striking distance. A small fish may dash into the kelp and escape from one predator, only to be taken by another.

Blood sea stars (above) appear to spawn on tiptoe; in reality, they shed eggs and sperm from holes between their arms. Fishes from sarcastic fringeheads (left) to sharks of many varieties call the kelp forest home.

LIFE ALONG THE ROCKY REEF:
Holding fast to the ocean floor

he rocky reef to which the great kelp stands cling is often encrusted with marine life several inches thick. The colors displayed by these encrusting plants and animals range from brilliant to literally fluorescent. Pigments within the tissues of certain anemones, nudibranchs, and algae actually absorb blue or green ambient light and then fluoresce into spectacular reds and oranges. Swimming over the reef within a kelp forest is much like floating over a field of precious stones illuminated by a blacklight.

The predators that hunt within the caves and canyons of the reef often use cryptic coloration or camouflage as a hunting strategy. Like land animals that employ colors and patterns as camouflage, reef predators must blend with the sizzling colors of their surroundings. So they tend to display equally dazzling wardrobes and textures.

So well disguised is the spotted scorpionfish that it may be nearly invisible

A small octopus pauses to adjust its coloring and texture to match the coralline algae, rocks, and spiral gill worms on which it dances.

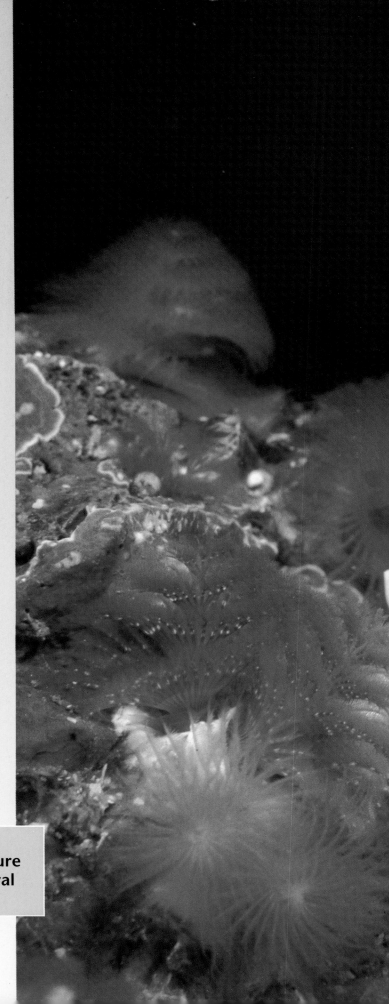

Whose face only a mother could love?

A moray eel, that's who. This villainous-looking fellow smells rather than sees its way to its prey. In its rocky lair along the kelp forest reef, the moray hangs out, lurking patiently for octopus and fishes. Then it strikes with razor-blade teeth and jaws of iron. What does a soft creature like an octopus do to escape? James Bond-like, it releases a spectacular cloud of ink at the scene.

More than a diversionary smoke-screen, the ink cloud contains an anesthetic which temporarily deadens the moray eel's ability to smell.

In their long lives, morays can grow to be six feet in length, and as much as one foot in diameter. That's a lot of ugly. But looks are deceiving. Divers say that despite its appearance, a moray eel is a timid soul, more pussycat than killer of the kelp forest.

to a diver a few feet away. This foot-long hunter lies motionless on the bottom among the encrusted rocks, looking like just another rock. When a small fish ventures close, the scorpionfish reacts with lightning quickness, sucking the fish into its mouth and swallowing it whole. Because the dorsal spines of the scorpionfish are armed and deadly with venom, divers need to look very carefully before touching the reef.

Many other bottom-dwelling fishes – turbots, rockfishes, blennies, sculpins, and others – use camouflage both to hunt and to avoid being hunted. A number of invertebrates adopt this strategy as well. Decorator crabs use their claws to plant algae, anemones, and sponges on their backs and legs. Until they move, they are almost impossible to spot.

The Grand Master of camouflage has to be the octopus. Not only does it take on the color of the reef or the sand it resides upon, the octopus mimics the texture and shape of its surroundings as well. How long does it take for this transformation? The blink of an eye. One minute you see a bright red octopus sitting on a reef. The next second: gone. Its skin, loaded with special pigment cells called chromatophores, make quick changes possible. You may not think so to look at it, but the octopus is a mollusk that traded the protection of a shell for speed and mobility. To compensate for its vulnerability, the octopus developed a repertoire of camouflage techniques.

In addition, the octopus can squirt clouds of ink at its attackers, including its greatest enemy, the moray eel. Although the eel has poor eyesight, its sense of smell is

FOOD ON THE REEF:
Anemones, bat stars, snails, cup corals, and other small filter feeders wait for currents to deliver dinner. What do they eat? Plankton and drift kelp. Because of their ability to sting prey and digest it with ease, anemones are meat-eaters that will take on prey from crabs to large fishes.

acute. When a moray attacks an octopus, the mollusk releases its ink cloud. More than a smoke-screen, the ink contains an anesthetic which deadens the eel's olfactory senses. If the octopus manages to escape, the eel cannot smell the octopus well enough to pursue. In such encounters, the octopus often loses an arm or two while fleeing. Like other invertebrates, it has the handy ability to regrow lost limbs through a process called autotomy.

Although using cryptic coloration to "disappear" is effective both as an ambush and an escape strategy, many reef species use hot colors to advertise their presence. Nudibranchs, for instance. Despite their soft bodies, these sea slugs flaunt colors brighter than the gaudiest fishing lure. Rather than "Come eat me," these colors say: "If you eat me, you'll be very sorry!" Most nudibranchs have an extremely unpleasant taste. Some are poisonous. Many taste bad and sting.

Several species of fishes use coloration to trumpet their presence. The Catalina goby shimmers with neon-bright blues and oranges. And the garibaldi, fiery orange as a Hawaiian sunset, seems to have no worries at all. It enjoys legal protection from humans because it is pretty and not very good to eat. And it is not bothered by fishy predators, either.

Garibaldi make their nests on the reef within the kelp forest. That is, the male does. First he chooses a suitable nesting place on the side of a rock. Next, he spends a few days removing all of the growth from the rock except for several species of small red algae, which he prunes into a lush circular patch about 18 inches across. Then the male sets out to show the females of his species what a good job he has done. He swims several feet above the nest. When a prospective mate passes near, he clucks three times, dashing toward the nest in hopes the female will follow. When his nest succeeds in impressing a female, she lays her eggs in the algae patch.

After laying her eggs, she swims off once again, leaving the parenting to the male. He fertilizes the eggs, then spends the next two weeks looking after them, keeping the nest clean, and protecting it from predators. Once the baby garibaldi hatch and drift away, the male takes little notice. His attention is still on the nest, which he often continues to guard for several days. Baby garibaldi are even more beautiful than their parents. Their deep orange bodies are punctuated with iridescent blue polka-dots.

Most of the encrusting life living on the reef looks plantlike but is actually animal. You could easily mistake an anemone for a flower blossom, a lacy gorgonian coral for a bush, or a finger sponge for a succulent plant. Many of these animals spend their lives anchored to one spot. Although not very quick or dangerous, these often-hungry beauties are predators nonetheless. Anemones and gorgonian corals wait for plankton and other small prey to drift into their tentacles. Tiny stinging structures called nematocysts in the tentacles then harpoon the prey.

The nematocysts of corals and anemones also protect from potential predators. But this protection is not entirely foolproof. In fact, to the rainbow nudibranch, nothing sounds more tasty than the stinging tentacles of the tube anemone! This sea slug makes a career of crawling from one anemone to the next, inching up the tube, and lunching on the tentacles. Rather than digest the nematocysts, it moves them internally to its gills. There they remain, alive and armed, protecting the nudibranch from anything foolish enough to tackle it.

Its burning bush beauty resembles an exquisite land plant, but the gorgonian coral is an animal, and a hungry one at that. Each slender stalk is a high-rise home to thousands of tiny polyps, each of which waits for small planktonic animals to float within snapping distance. Just like its anemone cousins, gorgonian polyps are equipped with nematocysts or minute stinging structures.

Courtship in slow motion: enormous swirling schools of bat rays, some with wingspans of five feet or more, meet and mate in the kelp forest clearings. This rarely-seen phenomenon occurs each summer.

LIFE IN THE KELP FOREST CLEARINGS:
Sandy dwellers & stalkers

Ocean bottom not covered with rocky reef is generally covered with sand. Fields of sand exist between kelp forests and as clearings within forests. Often, the outer edge of the kelp forest marks the edge of rocky reef and the beginning of a sand plain that slopes down to the deeper sea. Whereas kelp forests may be compared to redwoods or rainforests on land, the sandy bottom is much like terrestrial desert. In the same way that deserts appear lifeless, the sandy bottom conceals many living surprises. Quantities of fishes and invertebrates conceal themselves in the sand, waiting for passing prey. Halibut, angel sharks, turbot, and flounder bury themselves up to the eyes. When a likely fish passes within reach, they strike upwards, quick and effective as a lightning bolt.

Other animals use the sand to hide from predators. The red octopus hides beneath the sand or in worm holes, emerging at night to forage. Heart urchins, some sea stars, and cusk eels also remain buried during the day, coming out at night to feed as well.

Being entirely buried in sand doesn't offer complete protection from being eaten, however. Many sharks and rays have organs that are sensitive to electrical fields. They find prey by sensing the weak electrical field created by another animal's circulatory system. Horn sharks, bat rays, sting rays, and thornback rays all cruise the sandy bottom in this manner, honing in on completely buried prey.

Like habitats we are more familiar with, the kelp forest experiences what we might call seasons. Kelp animals and plants go through cycles of birth,

COMMON GROUND:
What do a lizardfish, an octopus, and a hermit crab have in common? All of them use the sandy plains of the kelp forest clearings to hide and to hunt. Other species, such as squid and rays, find the sand ideal for courtship, mating, and egg-laying. Large predators like sharks work the sandy plain like metal detectors, spotting completely buried prey via special sensing organs.

WEIRD WEAPONS:
Rainbow nudibranchs and many other sea slugs thrive on deadly foods. They attack tube anemones, eating just the beautiful tentacles, which are full of nematocysts or stinging structures. Once swallowed, the sea slug transfers them where they can do the most good: to its feathery gills, where they serve to protect the nudibranch. The now-defenseless anemone suffers a futher indignity: the rainbow lays its eggs on the outside of its tube.

growth, dormancy, and decay, much as terrestrial species do, giving a new aspect to the kelp forest at different times of the year.

In early spring, for example, the sand environment at the outer edge of the kelp forest comes alive. Millions of deep-water squid rise from the depths of the open ocean to spawn in the sand at the forest's edge. In about 100 feet of water, enormous schools of male and female squid meet and mate almost simultaneously. After mating, the female squid produces an egg case nearly half the length of her body. She carries it to the bottom, where she digs deep into the sand, depositing an anchor to hold the egg case in place above the sand.

Soon, millions upon millions of egg cases crowd the sandy floor, leaving little room for more. Sheer numbers force latecomer female squid to anchor their egg cases to clusters of other eggs. Eventually, a blanket of squid eggs as much as two feet thick covers many acres of sandy bottom adjacent to the kelp forest.

After spawning, all the adult squid die. By the millions! Perhaps it is for this reason that the squid show absolutely

no fear of predators during mating and egg laying. For the squid, time is short and they have only one thing on their minds. Fear of being eaten becomes a minor concern.

For those animals who dine on squid, squid spawning time is a non-stop feeding orgy. Sea lions and harbor seals, sharks and bat rays, lobsters and crabs, dolphins and whales all gather to enjoy the easy pickings. No matter how many and voracious their number, the predators cannot consume all the squid. They try their utmost, but thousands of dead and dying squid soon litter the bottom surrounding the acres of egg cases. Then smaller predators and scavengers get their chance to stuff themselves with squid. Both predators and scavengers ignore the squid eggs. Either they don't taste good or the diners are so full of squid that they have no appetite left. Whatever the reason, the squid eggs are left to hatch unmolested.

Each squid case contains about 200 individual eggs. In two weeks or so, the eggs mature and the baby squid hatch out to drift away as part of the plankton. Where these young squid go, what they do during their first two or three years of life, is virtually unknown. In three years, however, they invariably return to the kelp forest to spawn like their parents and begin the cycle anew.

In early summer, long after the baby squid have vanished into the open ocean, bat rays accumulate in great numbers along the outer edge of the kelp forest. In the

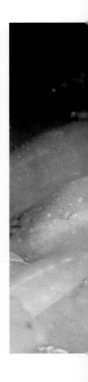

What floats like a butterfly, stings like a bee?

A giant pelagic jellyfish, that's what. This beautiful drifter is sometimes carried by currents from ocean depths to nearshore waters. Odd as it sounds, its fearsome tentacles make spicy eating for the gastronomically bold garibaldi fishes of the kelp forest. This jellyfish serves as another sort of meal ticket. Tiny jack fishes hide among its 15-foot tentacles for protection. A coating on their bodies renders them resistant to stings. Other creatures share symbiotic relationships with jellyfish. Certain crabs, for example, dine on the plankton-impregnated mucus they produce. Much about jellyfishes remains mysterious. This species, for instance, was unknown to biologists until it was photographed in the kelp forest and dead specimens began washing up on California shores in 1989.

evening, these beautiful bird-like creatures, some with wingspans of five feet or more, form enormous swirling schools. Seen from below, these schools look like huge flocks of birds, their great diamond shapes circling in a column of rising air beneath a thundercloud. Thousands of bat rays eventually join the schools, where males and females spend at least a week playing the mating game.

Beginning in the evening, and continuing into the night, bat rays court. The male swims beneath the female, caressing her stomach with his back. Often she rejects him, darting away with a rapid beat of her wings. If and when he finally wins her affection, they mate. In the morning, the rays settle into the sand, wingtip to wingtip, for as far as the eye can see. All day they rest in the sand, waiting for the sun to set so they may begin once again their long and tender courtship patterns. Much about bat ray reproduction remains a mystery. We do know, however, that the females give birth to live young.

PEACEFUL COEXISTENCE:

Tiny jack fish and even tinier crabs cuddle within the fearsome velvety bell of the jellyfish, protected from its poison by coatings on shell or skin. What does the jellyfish get out of this association? We know little about this and other aspects of this hypnotic creature.

Kelp forest enemies & allies

Just as weather affects conditions on land, it also influences the environment under the sea. Storms, for example, produce strong winds. Wind blowing across the ocean surface creates waves. Underwater, the waves passing overhead are felt as surge. When a large wave moves through the kelp forest, the water in the forest rushes back and forth. The larger the wave, the stronger the surge and the deeper it penetrates. How violent is the result? Strong surge feels like a hurricane blowing one direction for 30 seconds, then the opposite direction for the same amount of time. In strong surge, a diver can be tumbled across the ocean bottom like a tumbleweed in a whirlwind. Large winter storms can devastate the kelp forest. Especially severe ones produce waves and surge so powerful that holdfasts are torn from the reef. At times like these, entire forests are ripped loose and thrown onto the beach. Occasionally, tremendous storms hit the coast, destroying nearly every stand of kelp forest for hundreds of miles.

Such storms seem tragic. But they are a temporary tragedy for the kelp forest habitat. As soon as the storm passes and the sun comes out, kelp plants begin to germinate again on the reef. If conditions are good, the forests will return to their former lushness in less than a year.

Warm water poses another threat to Macrocystis forests. An oceanic phenomenon known as El Niño occasionally causes water temperatures to rise along parts

Harbor seals and other pinnipeds occasionally use the kelp forest as a hunting ground, but mainly it serves as a safe hideout spot from their most serious enemies, the sharks. Seals and sea lions nap in the world's best waterbed: amid the fronds of the kelp forest canopy.

of the Pacific Coast. In 1982, for example, a powerful El Niño struck the kelp forests of this area. Water temperatures rose ten degrees above normal, and the warm water was poor in the nutrients that sustain kelp. This El Niño persisted for three years. Even after weather conditions returned to normal, damage was so severe that it took years before the kelp forests returned to their former majesty.

Natural events like El Niño occur every few decades, scientists believe. But atmospheric warming of our planet due to the greenhouse effect is intensifying because of human intervention. This trend may create stronger and more frequent El Niños in the future.

The greatest natural enemy of the kelp forest? The sea urchin, particularly the purple species. Populations of these urchins sometimes bloom, producing giant moving fronts of the prickly animals. Purple urchins have an insatiable appetite for kelp. An urchin front can march through a kelp forest, devouring every holdfast in its path and setting the entire forest adrift.

Before modern humans began exploiting fisheries resources along the Pacific Coast, the balance between purple urchins and kelp was maintained by several predators with a good-sized appetite for urchins. Sea otters and sheephead fish once fed on urchins all along the coast, keeping the populations in check. In southern California, however, sea otters were eliminated from the ecosystem long ago. Today they are endangered even within their northern California range. The amiable sheephead has been fished so heavily that its influence on urchin populations is now minimal.

Without predators to keep them under control, purple urchin populations explode. In some areas, the density of purple urchins exceeds 300 per square yard. Like army ants in slow motion, they move through the kelp forest, devouring all brown algae in their path. In their wake, little more than barren rock remains.

As noted earlier, a commercial use for red sea urchins has been developed in recent years. Divers who once dived for abalone now dive for red urchins, exporting the roe to Asian countries. Because purple urchins have smaller roe, a market for them has been slow to develop. As red urchins

DINING ON DIAMONDS: Divers in the kelp forest still find impressively sized lobsters, but legal-sized abalone are getting rare as gemstones. In years past, a limit of abalone could be lifted off one rock. Today it takes an hour's diving to find one.

become scarcer, however, divers and their customers may turn to purple urchins as a replacement. Perhaps then man's influence on the kelp forest will help realign nature's balance rather than upset it.

Macrocystis plants contain a very useful compound called algin. Acting as an emulsifying, stabilizing, and gelling agent, algin prevents liquids from separating and makes liquid foods thicker and smoother. It's found in ice cream, beer, salad dressing, canned foods, and hundreds of edibles and is widely used in industry for cosmetics and much more. The paper and ink on these pages – even the clothes you're wearing – probably contain algin. The only company in the U.S. to harvest kelp for algin is Kelco Company of Southern California. Since 1929, this San Diego firm has used large vessels to pass over mature kelp forests, trimming off the top three feet of kelp canopy. These harvesters gather up to 600 tons of kelp in as little as eight hours. Because only the tops are trimmed, the submerged plant remains intact and the forest undamaged. In a few months, the canopy can again be harvested without harm.

In other parts of the world, kelp is used by humans as mulch and fertilizer. And the scarcity of wild abalone has led to a breakthrough in aquaculture: abalone farming. These farms also use quantities of harvested kelp to feed the mollusks.

Kelp forests attract and harbor many species of fish and shellfish, making this a key habitat for commercial fishermen. Lobsters, abalone, and red urchins are all species dependent upon the kelp forest habitat. Commercial fishermen use gill nets to catch a variety of kelp forest fish, such as white sea bass, halibut, soupfin sharks, and angel sharks. Unfortunately, many of the species caught in these nets have no commercial value. Called "incidental kill," these animals are thrown back as waste. Often the incidental kill greatly exceeds the harvest of marketable fish.

Diving in an area where a gill net has been used can be a heart-breaking experience. One year during the bat ray

mating season, I swam out into such an area. The ocean floor was littered with hundreds of dead bat rays, caught unintentionally, then killed and discarded as valueless.

You probably find this waste as disturbing as I do. But the blame cannot be laid entirely upon commercial fishermen. Today's fisherman tries to make his living in an unhappy triangle of circumstances. Worldwide there is more public demand for seafood. More competition from fishermen of all nationalities and degrees of scrupulousness. And less fish. Always

Without predators to hold them in check, urchins may achieve a density of 300 animals per square yard. When that happens, the mass of urchins becomes a front, a plague that moves through the kelp forest, grinding everything in its path. Holdfasts are sheared off at the roots, setting the entire kelp forest adrift.

less fish. What's needed? A more informed public. People who insist on fish and shellfish that are caught without wasteful killing, and who put their money where their convictions are.

Quite possibly the kelp forest's biggest fans are SCUBA divers and snorkelers. Hundreds of thousands of sport divers explore the forests every year. Most experienced divers agree: no undersea habitat is more beautiful. For divers with a taste for seafood, there are lobsters, abalone, rock scallops, white sea bass, halibut, and more. Many divers, however, venture underwater to hunt for pictures with a camera or simply to hunt for adventure. Kelp forests generate an unlimited supply of these things. Swimming through a forest of 100-foot kelp trees is like having wings and flying through huge redwoods. In the subdued golden light, all sorts of unusual creatures may be found. Brilliant orange garibaldi are friendly and quick to feed from your hand. Harbor seals follow you about, pugnaciously popping out from behind kelp fronds to give you a start. Sea lions dart through the kelp, playfully blowing bubbles at you, nipping harmlessly at your fins. And schools of bat rays and jack mackerel flash overhead in a ballet of synchronization.

In contrast to the growing number of terrestrial habitats that have been degraded or chopped to pieces by human development, the kelp forest remains essentially wild. Even in forests frequented by divers, you won't find a human footprint, a trail that must be followed, or a park ranger directing traffic. Those of us who dive these forests are lucky beyond belief. We see a vast wilderness, invisible from our workaday world, yet close enough to visit often. Once you put on your diving gear, you enter a magical place where you might see creatures still undescribed by science, where you can find adventure and solitude.

The kelp forest remains a true wilderness habitat. But it's not immune to pressures and pollution exerted by increasing human populations. From outer space, this planet is blue, it is ocean. What we discard into the sea does not vanish. What we do to its creatures comes back to haunt us. Most humans will never see this remote and golden wilderness firsthand. But the need for its protection remains urgent. Think of it as environmental insurance. Or as a legacy for our children, and the children of the sea otter, and the rockfish, and the squid.

A WASTE-FREE SEA:
Too many gill nets catch numerous fish that are trashed as 'incidental kill.' Carelessly jettisoned fishing gear strangles seals. Plastic six-pack loops wash out to sea to become death warrants for birds, whales, and other creatures. Keeping the sea and the kelp forest free of human debris is a big step toward saving our planet.

More about Kelp Forests

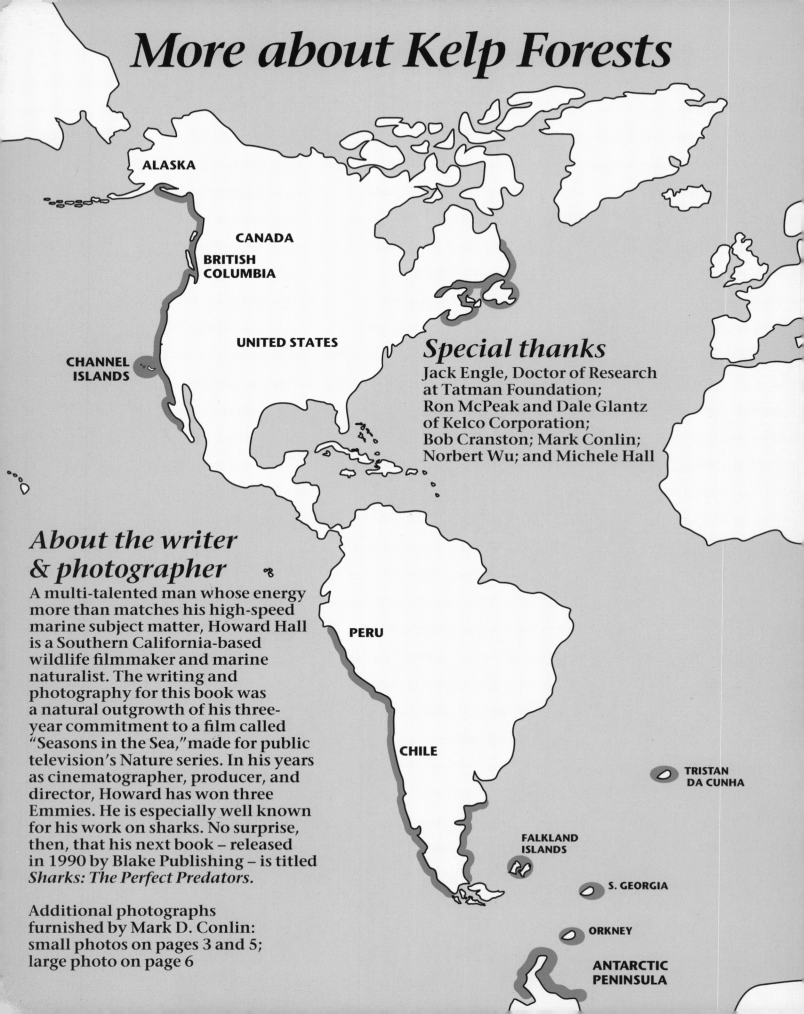

ALASKA

CANADA

BRITISH
COLUMBIA

UNITED STATES

CHANNEL
ISLANDS

PERU

CHILE

TRISTAN
DA CUNHA

FALKLAND
ISLANDS

S. GEORGIA

ORKNEY

ANTARCTIC
PENINSULA

Special thanks

Jack Engle, Doctor of Research
at Tatman Foundation;
Ron McPeak and Dale Glantz
of Kelco Corporation;
Bob Cranston; Mark Conlin;
Norbert Wu; and Michele Hall

About the writer
& photographer

A multi-talented man whose energy
more than matches his high-speed
marine subject matter, Howard Hall
is a Southern California-based
wildlife filmmaker and marine
naturalist. The writing and
photography for this book was
a natural outgrowth of his three-
year commitment to a film called
"Seasons in the Sea," made for public
television's Nature series. In his years
as cinematographer, producer, and
director, Howard has won three
Emmies. He is especially well known
for his work on sharks. No surprise,
then, that his next book – released
in 1990 by Blake Publishing – is titled
Sharks: The Perfect Predators.

Additional photographs
furnished by Mark D. Conlin:
small photos on pages 3 and 5;
large photo on page 6

Diving the kelp forests

BEST IN THE WEST:
• Channel Islands National Marine Sanctuary
OTHER LIKELY SPOTS:
• Puget Sound and Barkley Sound, Washington
• Monterey Bay • Point Lobos State Reserve
• Big Sur • Santa Barbara • Palos Verdes peninsula
• Laguna Beach • La Jolla Underwater Park
• Point Loma, San Diego
• Baja California as far south as San Ignacio Lagoon
• For armchair divers: the multi-species 3-story kelp
  forest display at the Monterey Bay Aquarium

Recommended books & films

• *The Amber Forest*
by McPeak, Glantz and Shaw
• *California Marine Life*
by Marty Snyderman
• "Seasons in the Sea,"
a film on California marine life
and the kelp forest habitat, filmed
and produced by Howard Hall
for public television's Nature series.

SOUTH AFRICA

AUSTRALIA

TASMANIA

NEW ZEALAND

ANTARCTICA

MAP NOT TO SCALE

Call or write for other books in our growing nature series:

Habitats:
Tidepools ❖ *The Kelp Forest* ❖ *Icebergs & Glaciers*
Tropical Rainforests ❖ *Coral Reefs*

Marine Life:
A Raft of Sea Otters ❖ *Seals & Sea Lions*
A Pod of Gray Whales ❖ *A Pod of Killer Whales*
Humpback Whales ❖ *Sharks*

Bird Life:
Hawks, Owls & Other Birds of Prey
Parrots, Macaws & Cockatoos
A Dazzle of Hummingbirds

SILVER BURDETT PRESS

© 1995 Silver Burdett Press
Published by Silver Burdett Press.
A Simon & Schuster Company
299 Jefferson Road,
Parsippany, NJ 07054
Printed in the United States of America